Christians Deserve Orgasms Too!

Christians Deserve Orgasms Too

The Things No One Told You About Sex

By: Chrystle Jones

Pursuit of Destiny
Lifestyle Publishing

Copyright © 2022 Chrystle Jones

All rights reserved

All rights reserved. No part of this book may be reproduced in any form or by an electronic or mechanical means, including information storage and retrieval systems, without permission in writing from the publisher, except by a reviewer who may quote brief passages in a review.

ISBN 9780578398709 (Paperback)
First Edition

Pursuit of Destiny Lifestyle Publishing
2541 N. Dale Mabry HWY #267
Tampa, FL 33604

Acknowledgements

This book is dedicated to my amazing husband. His support empowers me to be so many things I've never even imagined. One of my greatest honors and privileges in life is being your wife.

To my friend Leslie W., the first person I told I wanted to write a book about sex, 7 years ago. Thank you for being a non-judgmental listening ear that challenges me to dig deeper.

CONTENTS

CHAPTER 1: Deconstructing To Reconstruct — 9
CHAPTER 2: Problematic Thinking — 15
CHAPTER 3: The Orgasm — 24
CHAPTER 4: Erogenous Zones — 38
CHAPTER 5: Intimacy — 47
CHAPTER 6: Conversations About Sex — 55
CHAPTER 7: Set The Mood — 65
CHAPTER 8: Best I Ever Had — 71
CHAPTER 9: Oral Sex — 83
CHAPTER 10: Moisture 101 — 92
CHAPTER 11: A Guided Tour — 98
CHAPTER 12: Sex Positions — 107
CHAPTER 13: Introducing New Things — 113
CHAPTER 14: Tips And Tricks — 120
CHAPTER 15: Healthy Sex Habits — 126
CONCLUSION — 141

CHAPTER 1

Deconstructing to Reconstruct

Growing up in the Christian community I was taught that sex is bad, that it is the ultimate sin, and that I should avoid it at all costs. This was the beginning of my very unhealthy journey into celibacy because it was based on fear: fear of pregnancy, fear of sexually transmitted diseases, and fear of Hell. At every level, I had to find a way to suppress my ever-increasing desire for intimate moments with the opposite sex. A phone call could lead to an inappropriate conversation, and a simple kiss could be a gateway to the vagina.

The issue is that so much time is spent learning why you shouldn't have sex that no one knows what to do when it comes time to be vulnerable and intimate with someone you care about. What's more, no practical tools were taught for dealing with the feelings and emotions that arise during puberty. Ignoring your feelings, attempting to pray them away, or asking God to remove your sex drive entirely, are NOT practical solutions, and they do not work. God is not going around removing sex drives because He created them!

When it came to sex, I felt like I got the short end of the stick as a woman. My attempts to live a celibate life not only failed, but also proved problematic when I married because I had spent so many years suppressing my natural desires and judging myself every time I gave in. I never learned to be comfortable with my own body, let alone accept someone else's. As much as I thought I was getting the short end of the stick, imagine my surprise when I discovered that men are also frustrated when they enter a sexual relationship and realize they lack the tools necessary to understand how to please a woman. Everything hurts her, and despite the fact that you were both looking forward to this intimate moment, she doesn't seem to be enjoying it as much as you do or at all.

Like many others in the Christian community, I was subconsciously programmed to dislike sex and view it as nasty. For some inexplicable reason, that was the best attempt to convince people not to have premarital sex. The truth is that it didn't work. It only made it that much more difficult to have healthy sexual relationships when the time was right. Because sex was not discussed, we have a plethora of men and women who are dissatisfied or selfish in the bedroom when they enter into a sexual relationship. I'm not suggesting that everyone should have as much sex as they can, as many people have had numerous sexual partners but have never had or given an orgasm. The solution is to talk about sex.

Some of you who have this book are thinking, "I can't believe she wrote a book about sex." I don't blame you; we've been conditioned to avoid the subject. But don't worry, you've come to the right place to learn about sex. Not the spiritual perspective mentioned for 20 minutes in some churches' marriage seminars or a dedicated marriage counseling session once everything hits the fan, but the fun stuff you really want to know that will ignite your sex life, help you connect or reconnect with your partner, and blow their mind so you both want more of each other.

This book is not a deep dive into my personal experiences; rather, it is a resource based on research from various sources. Let's talk about how to overcome the discomfort of being naked in front of someone, how to feel comfortable touching your partner, and positions to ensure sex is pleasurable whether your man is well-endowed or not, because a slight turn of the hips can mean the difference between pain and pleasure, or feeling nothing and feeling everything. This book will force many of you to reconsider what you've been taught, or even what you've assumed because you haven't been taught anything at all. I'd like to encourage you to embrace it. Do not take everything I say as law, because every relationship is unique and personal, just as your relationship with God should be. Except for orgasms, which are a must, there are no hard and fast rules or requirements. Consider this book to be a catalyst to get you started.

If I said I wanted to bake a cake without instructions, even though I'd never baked a cake in my life, it probably wouldn't go well. I might know to put the flour in a bowl and, by chance, figure out an edible recipe, but how long would that take, and what are the chances of that happening? This is exactly what has occurred in the Christian community. People have sex and believe they're doing it correctly because they've been doing it for a long time. Wrong. You may be baking a bad cake over and over. There's a reason some cakes are moist while others are dry. Some are memorable, while others you'll never eat again. It's because some bakers know what they're doing, while others think they do but don't. I hope you understand that I'm not talking about bakers and cakes, but rather about sex.

I've heard countless stories concerning brides who didn't know what to do on their wedding night or men who couldn't figure out where to put "it." People who had to endure embarrassing moments, and women who described their first time as excruciatingly painful - all because the Christian community refuses to talk about sex. Let's talk about it, mind-blowing, earth-shattering, orgasmic sex. The number of sexual partners you've had has nothing to do with the quality of sex you will have with your partner. Whether you're still a virgin preparing for your big moment, or simply not as experienced as your partner, you have the chance to have the best sex ever. Communication is the key to having great sex.

CHAPTER 2

Problematic Thinking

Sex is bad. The problematic statement that has echoed through churches around the world for countless centuries. The lie that launches millions of Christian men and women into marriage under the pretense that sex suddenly becomes good once you're married. The problem is that for many, sex doesn't become good when they get married. Mostly for the reason that many still don't know what they are doing, and also because the mindset that has been used to frame sex for so many years has become ingrained in the experience before it even begins. The first step to a healthy sex life is to eradicate the lie that sex isn't good. Sex is good. Whether you're married or not doesn't change that truth; whether or not you know what you are doing does.

This lie must be confronted head-on because an orgasm, particularly in women, is more than just physical. Did you know that orgasms can be triggered solely by thoughts? You can have an orgasm alone in your room, without anyone touching you. Many couples are perplexed as to why their sex life is good but not great, and there are several causes. One of the main reasons is you need more orgasms! When a man or woman has an orgasm, they experience euphoria that makes them want to have sex again and again. Without orgasm sex is like having a piece of cake that was good at the time, but you wouldn't go out of your way to have again.

The problem is that as an adult, you almost always have to go out of your way to have sex due to busy work schedules, children to care for, or any number of other factors. Normally, a man reaches orgasm during sex, but for women, this achievement seems to be elusive, which is one of several reasons why women are less interested in sex. If you want to know how to make your partner want more sex, make sure she has an orgasm. I'm going to look at sex from a variety of perspectives, but first I need to talk about women. Men, keep reading because it will shed a lot of light on why you might be having trouble with intimacy in your relationship.

Whether or not your partner was raised in the Christian church, but especially if she was, she was most likely taught one or more of the following lies: Any interest in sex makes her promiscuous; the primary reason for a woman to have sex is to serve her husband; she should try to pray her sex drive away; if she succeeds, it's a sign of how holy she is, and she shouldn't be sexy. Literally level 10 toxic information for so many reasons. This is how it all looks when she's in a sexual relationship.

You make an advance, and she acts as if she doesn't like it because it makes her appear promiscuous when she expresses a desire for sex. Despite the fact that she is in a committed relationship, that is ingrained in her mind. You wonder why she seems inactive during sex rather than opening up and engaging in the moment, and she believes she isn't supposed to enjoy the moment too much because her body is really only there for your pleasure. You may wonder why she never makes sexual advances, and the truth is that she has spent most of her life attempting to make sex a nonexistent thought through prayer and repression in order to be "pure," so sex is not a priority for her at all. If you're wondering why she only wants to have sex with the lights turned off and under the covers, it's because she was never taught that it was acceptable to think of herself as sexy and desirable. So even if you say you love her naked body, she's still trying to wrap her head around you seeing her naked body.

How are we going to deal with this? First, we have conversations in which we dismantle that type of thinking. Second, orgasms! Did you know that some women have never experienced an orgasm? I'm not referring to virgins; rather, I'm referring to women who have been having sex for years. It's not always because her partner is sexually inexperienced; sometimes it's because she doesn't know enough about her body to express her desires, and her partner doesn't know enough about the female anatomy to provide her with what she requires. This leads to both of them attempting to obtain what they desire by any means. A healthy sexual relationship is one in which **BOTH** people do everything possible to fulfill their partner's needs.

We often point out women with low sex drives, but there are also relationships in which men are unbiased toward sex because it's highly unsatisfying. The woman they're with doesn't make it exciting at all. Ladies, who taught you how to satisfy your man orally? Or have you been taught that Christian ladies do not do that? Maybe you are doing all the right things once the moment begins but he is the one that is too distracted to engage and you need some new tools in your kit to help you understand how to get him in the mood. Which you would be open to but, you have been programmed into refraining from making sexual advances toward your partner so doing so just feels awkward? It may sound strange, but women are taught from a young age how to be a woman: quiet, modest, and devoid of flatulence. Then, when they queef for the first time during sex, they feel bewildered and humiliated, wondering where it came from and how to stop it. Queefing, by the way, is simply air escaping from the vagina during intercourse. It does not smell like anything, but it may indicate that more lubricant is required.

This book is about sex. For that reason I chose a bold title that includes the word orgasm, and as a Christian, you shouldn't be ashamed to have a book with orgasm in the title because God created sex. Understanding your sexuality does not require you to have sex. It allows you to be knowledgeable enough about it and the pleasure you should experience from it so you no longer end up with the short end of the sex stick when the time is right! It means you won't merely lie down and surrender your body to your companion as a sacrifice or obligation, but that you understand you were designed to enjoy sex. How can we go from an uninformed group of individuals to an educated group of people ready to experience the best sex ever? First, we need to talk about what an orgasm is.

Exercise 1

False information concerning sex has been circulating in the Christian community and has damaged relationships long before my time. Although in most cases this information was given with the best of intentions, it's important to grow beyond what was said as more understanding arises. Let's do a brief exercise to move past these thoughts.

What things have you been taught about sex that have prevented you from enjoying your sex life or trying new things?

_____
_____
_____
_____

What are some things you were taught or believed about sex that didn't make sense and you couldn't find a reference in the Bible?

What can you do to actively work on giving sex a new value and mindset so that it's pleasurable for you both physically and mentally?

CHAPTER 3

The Orgasm

The definition of an orgasm, according to Merriam-Webster, is: *intense or paroxysmal excitement. Especially: the rapid, pleasurable release of neuromuscular tensions at the height of sexual arousal, that is usually accompanied by the ejaculation of semen in the male and by vaginal contractions in the female.* This definition omits the fact that women can ejaculate. Female ejaculation differs from the fluid felt when a woman becomes moist due to arousal. However, that fluid is critical for both parties to have a satisfying sexual experience. Also, oxytocin and dopamine are released during an orgasm, resulting in emotions of enjoyment and intimacy. If you and your lover are estranged, orgasms are a terrific way to reconnect.

The Male Orgasms

Did you know there are different types of male orgasms? The "standard" male orgasm is one in which ejaculation occurs as a result of stimulation of the penis and scrotum. It is important to note that orgasm and male ejaculation are two distinct psychological processes, but they frequently occur together. The Standard male orgasm is typically obtained through penetrative sex, oral sex, or manually with the hand. The timeframe in which this type of orgasm occurs might range from 5 minutes to 30 minutes or longer.

If you're wondering why your partner isn't able to last longer, there are two possible explanations. The first is that he does not have enough sex. The more intimacy you and your partner share, the better he will be able to build stamina. It's easy to complain about unsatisfying intimacy, but sex is a team sport. If you only have sex once a week, the moment will almost certainly not last long enough for the woman to climax. A tip for building stamina is edging, which is a technique in which the male gets to the point just before ejaculation and then calms himself down to avoid a release. The second factor that causes a man to be unable to withhold release is premature ejaculation. This is when a man ejaculates involuntarily within 1-2 minutes of penetration. If this has been happening on a regular basis for at least six months, he should seek medical attention.

The next type of orgasm is one that your husband most likely experienced as a teenager. The notorious wet dream orgasm. Contrary to popular belief, this form of orgasm is not solely the result of romantic fantasies. This form of orgasm happens while you're sleeping and may or may not be followed by ejaculatory fluid and isn't always accompanied by an erection. If the dream is erotic in nature and he remembers it, the man may be thinking about an unfulfilled fantasy. If it does not violate your relationship's safe space, I would encourage you to discuss it with your partner. Later in this book, we'll discuss how to introduce new things into the bedroom.

The last type of male orgasm is a non-ejaculatory orgasm, which is induced by pudendal nerve stimulation and results in a pelvic floor orgasm. How are you going to get there? It all comes down to activating the nerves surrounding the anal entrance. For some men, this is entirely out of the question, but if you're intrigued, it can trigger numerous orgasms in a single sexual experience because ejaculation is absent. This stimulation can be provided by a finger, the mouth, or a toy. Similarly, the male G-spot corresponds to the prostate orgasm. This orgasm requires anal penetration with a finger or a toy, so it is another that may be off the table.

The Female Orgasm

Orgasms become even more complex when dealing with a woman. As I already stated, some women ejaculate while others do not. Female ejaculation can range from a modest bit of extra moisture to a heavy downpour. Some women even squirt from the Skene gland, which is present in all women, although not all women squirt.

Before you accuse your partner of faking it, check out the following physical indications that an orgasm has occurred or is going to occur: tightening of the vaginal walls. A woman's vaginal walls get considerably tighter when she is about to ejaculate, just as a man's genitals become harder when he is about to ejaculate. Her muscles contract, her toes curl, her pupils dilate, and her eyes roll back or close. Some women's legs become numb and their entire body trembles.

What happens during an orgasm depends on how it happens. There are various ways for a woman to experience orgasm, and I'll go over nine of them. You read that properly. The women's list is longer, and it's not because I'm biased. It's because, contrary to what you've heard, women are designed to enjoy sexual pleasure at a very high level. While we're at it, let's refute the myth that men are programmed to desire sex more than women. A more accurate statement would be that women are conditioned to suppress sexual desire more than men. In a sexual encounter, women can have an unlimited number of orgasms... Unlimited! Let's go over how to get these various types of orgasms in greater depth.

Clitoral orgasm is one of the more well-known types, and it is triggered by clitoris stimulation. The clitoris and the penis are quite similar. To begin with, the vagina is the canal utilized for intercourse and childbirth, but the clitoris is something different entirely. The clitoris, like an uncircumcised penis, has a foreskin. This is the clitoral hood, and it's meant to keep the clitoris safe. Furthermore, the clitoris can be as long as some penises! Although we only see a portion of it on top of the vaginal opening, the clitoris is around 4 inches long and shaped like a wishbone. When aroused, the clitoris grows just like a penis does! The clitoris is likewise similar to the tip of the penis in that it is the location where men and women are most "pleasure" sensitive. Women, on the other hand, have an advantage over men in that there are around 4,000 nerve endings at the tip of the penis, but 8,000 in the clitoris! So, if things aren't going as effectively as you'd want in the bedroom, it's possible that you're focusing on the wrong location, particularly the vaginal canal. Don't feel guilty; only approximately 25% of women climax from vaginal penetration alone. Please understand that there is nothing wrong with you or your partner; the focus just needs to be broadened.

The vagina changes during sex in the same way that the penis does. The vagina, not to be confused with the vulva, which refers to the labia, clitoris, and vaginal opening, changes during sex in the same way that the penis does. The penis changes from flaccid to long and hard. The vaginal canal grows in length and width. This type of orgasm can be achieved through oral sex, manual stimulation with fingers, a toy, or rubbing the penis on the clitoris. Some form of lubrication is required. We will go over lubrication options in greater detail in the chapter on moisture.

The g-spot orgasm follows. The g-spot is the prostate equivalent and is obtained via vaginal penetration. Some women have been on the verge of orgasm and were unaware of it due to a lack of education because they thought they needed to urinate. This is due to the g- spot's position in relation to the urethral sponge. When you have this sensation and stop because you think it's pee, you can give yourself the same unpleasant sensation that men have, known as "blue balls". It feels like a bad UTI/period cramp for about 30 seconds to 1 minute. The g- spot is located about 2 to 3 inches inside the vagina, toward the front. Yes, the rumors are true; size does not have to be a factor. Later, we'll discuss positions that make sex more pleasurable, as well as how to achieve orgasm with partners of all sizes.

When stimulation occurs in multiple areas at the same time, the result is a blended orgasm. Typically, a primary pleasure area, such as the clitoris or vaginal canal, is chosen, and then a secondary erogenous zone is engaged. Erogenous zones are areas of the body that can be touched to cause sexual arousal. We'll go over erogenous zones in greater detail later.

Anal orgasms are similar to male orgasms in that they can be induced through oral, manual, or toy stimulation. Remember when I said the clitoris is actually quite long, and we only see a small portion of it? Because it reaches from the front to the back of the vagina, the clitoris can be stimulated internally through anal penetration to achieve orgasm. This allows you to have a blended orgasm with just one tool.

Unless you want to experience the C-spot orgasm, size doesn't matter. The C-spot orgasm is a type of cervical orgasm that occurs when the penis comes into contact with the cervix, which is located at the back of the vaginal canal. For some, this is an incredible experience, but for others, it may be more pain than pleasure. Because this orgasm necessitates deep penetration, you must maintain a high level of arousal to avoid a painful experience.

Nipple orgasms are produced solely by stimulating the breast and nipples. The oxytocin released during nipple play can cause uterine contractions similar to those caused by vaginal and clitoral stimulation. This makes nipple stimulation ideal for foreplay, which is covered in detail in a separate chapter.

Because fantasy orgasms and wet dream orgasms are similar, I'll go over both. A fantasy orgasm is exactly what it sounds like. Sitting and having sexual thoughts to the point of orgasm. This could be a replay of your sexual highlight reel with your partner, or it could be thoughts about something you want to try with them. This orgasm can be achieved solely through thought. I do not recommend sitting around by yourself inducing orgasms through imagination; however, doing so while engaging in sexual intimacy with your partner can help you stay focused and achieve orgasm faster. Wet dream orgasms occur in the same way that they do in males.

Finally, there's the ejaculatory orgasm. This is an orgasm that occurs in tandem with ejaculation. Women's ejaculation fluid appears to be a watered-down milky material. This is also distinct from squirting, which, as previously said, is a liquid secreted by the Skene gland; all women have the gland, but not all women squirt.

I understand that this is a lot of information to take in, especially if you're beginning from scratch, but that's because there's a lot to learn about sex. When it comes to understanding how to please your current or future partner, there are numerous options to consider. You simply need the knowledge to determine what will work best for you. When it comes to orgasm types, don't feel obligated to accomplish one over the other. Each experience is unique, and as long as you achieve orgasm using at least one approach, you are on the right track. Conversations about sex to educate others are beneficial. Conversations about sex in order to make comparisons are harmful. Know the difference between the two and govern yourself accordingly. Let's take a break from learning and try some things out.

Exercise 2

When was the last time you and your partner spent some time getting to know each other's bodies? Not just turn off the lights and rush under the covers, but truly see each other? As strange as it may appear, it's a fantastic way to kickstart or reinvigorate an amazing sex life. Being comfortable with vulnerability in front of your partner is essential for amazing sex. Trust them to see your body and love it for what it is, even the flaws.

As I previously stated, orgasm can be achieved solely through thought, which speaks to the mental effort that goes into achieving an orgasm, particularly for a woman. The more relaxed and at ease she is, the more likely she is to have an orgasm.

To begin, set the tone. You want to be able to see each other clearly, but it's also important to set the mood, so dim the lights or simply light some candles to create a warm atmosphere.

Second, take turns taking each other's clothes off. Don't rush; take your time and appreciate each part of your body that emerges as you peel back the layers of clothing. Even if you are at ease in front of your partner, and as tempting as it may be to rush this moment, force yourself to slow down and look at each other. Turning on some slow music is a great way to keep the pace slow. However, if you can do it in silence, all the better to intensify the mood.

Third, express your preferences to your partner. Even when you're not in the throes of passion, expressing what you like about each other's bodies will make you both feel good. Touch that part of your partner's body as you tell each other what you like. If you want, you can use a gentle swipe, a passionate caress, or even a kiss. Get creative and touch them in the manner in which you want to experience them.

CHAPTER 4

Erogenous zones:

Have you ever sat in an airplane's cockpit? There are a plethora of controls and knobs. While preparing to take off, the pilots meticulously flip switches and push buttons, confirming with one another what has been accomplished at each stage of the process. The dashboard begins to light up as each knob is turned, and they become more prepared for flight. You and your partner are the pilots in the bedroom, and all those buttons, knobs, and switches are your erogenous zones. Just as pilots check in with one another as they approach takeoff, you should confirm with your partner that where you touch them and how you touch them is preparing them for takeoff.

Erogenous zones are useful for more than just foreplay. They contribute to the full-body orgasmic experience. Once you've determined where your partner prefers to be touched, you can use penetrative sex to heighten or extend their orgasm. In its most basic form, an erogenous zone is a region of the body that, when stimulated, causes sexual arousal. Because everyone is unique, there are numerous erogenous zones to explore with your partner. I'm going to list some areas that aren't as well-known as others in order to introduce you to new areas to try.

The neck is a hot spot that many know about but did you know kissing, touching, or even blowing on the neck was found to be more exciting than caressing the breast, buttocks, or other body parts in studies. An ice cube can also be used to engage this zone. The cool sensation followed by warm lips will stimulate the nerves in this area in novel ways. This is an excellent location for both men and women. Applying slight pressure with your lips or tongue will also deepen the pleasure. Consider it a French kiss on the neck.

The frenulum, like the clitoris, is a goldmine for pleasing a man. If you want to take your oral sex to the next level, lick him here! When you lift your tongue, you'll notice a thin piece of tissue connecting the bottom of your mouth to your tongue; that's called a frenulum. One of these is located at the bottom of the penis and connects the penis head to the shaft of the penis. If your man has been circumcised, it is visible; if he has not, you will need to pull back his foreskin to see it. You can stimulate this area even if you are not doing oral with a lubricated finger.

Have you ever kissed someone's earlobe? If you want to push your partner over the edge, start by whispering something sweet and sexy into their ear, then kiss or nibble on their earlobes. Take note that I said to kiss the earlobe. Most people will object if you insert your tongue into their ear canal. I'm not here to judge if that's your thing, but it should be a conversation or you'll ruin the mood. The earlobe, not the ear canal, is the part of the ear most commonly associated with arousal.

Due to them being so close to the main event, the inner thighs are an excellent erogenous zone. Stimulating this area with your mouth, tongue, or hands, reaching to the edge of where their genital area begins, then retreating down the thigh, will give them a buildup each time, increasing their desire for the moment. Want to take it to the next level? You can up the ante by adding whip cream, honey, or another delectable treat to lick away.

The lower stomach, between the belly button and the pubic area, is an excellent erogenous zone for getting things started. Light, soft touches stimulate this area well. You can gently glide over the area with your hands or a feather. When done correctly, you can actually stimulate a woman's g-spot. This is also an excellent location for experimenting with hot and cold stimulation. Orgasm is almost guaranteed if you successfully stimulate the g-spot and then immediately transition into oral sex.

The vulva's lips are referred to as the labia minora. The vulva is the exterior of the vaginal canal. Although it is tempting to go for the gold, the clitoris, stimulating the inner lips of the labia minora is far more rewarding. The key to engaging this area is to use a lot of lubricant. Rub the lubricated area with two fingers slightly separated from one another, increasing the speed. Add more, purchased or natural, lubricant as needed if your fingers or the area become dry.

The perineum is a spot that is often overlooked but is full of pleasure. This is the location of the pudendal nerve. This thin layer of skin lies between the anus and the genitals and can be ideal for those seeking variations that are not open to anal stimulation. This area can be stimulated with a lubricated finger, your mouth, or a vibrating toy. Finding ways to engage this area while having oral sex will result in a memorable orgasmic ending.

Including hot or cold sensations in the bedroom is an excellent way to boost sexual arousal. Cool sensations can be induced by using items such as ice, ice cream, cool whip, and blowing on your partner, among other things. Candle wax can be used to create hot or warm sensations; use caution it can get very hot; sip hot water and swish it around in your mouth before or use jalapenos. When placed on sensitive areas such as your nipples or lips, this spicy food can set off a chain reaction of sensations in your nerves. Just be sure you are ready because once you start the heat is on!

There are many erogenous zones, so I did not list them all, but there is one more that must be mentioned, and that is the brain. Your brain is the control center for what is stimulated. If you are not in the mood, you can be stimulated in the most amazing ways but limited to minimal enjoyment or no pleasure at all. In the following chapter, we'll talk about how to get in the mood and how to make the most of the moments you have with your partner!

Exercise 3

Experiment with something new! Because everyone is different, knowing what is and isn't on the table will help you and your partner create a safe space. Knowing they will not do anything you have already communicated is off the table allows you to relax and enjoy the moment more, which is especially important in the early stages of a relationship.

Fill out these questions with your partner to help create your safe space. There are no right or wrong answers, and it is fine if your partner is interested in something you are not; it is an opportunity for conversation. Later, we'll talk about how to introduce new things into the bedroom.

Tongue **yes or no**

Ears **yes or no**

Feet **yes or no**

Perineum **yes or no**

Neck **yes or no**

Lower back **yes or no**

Lubricants **all-natural (spit) or store-bought**

Food in the bedroom **yes or no**

Hot sensations **yes or no**

Cold sensations **yes or no**

CHAPTER 5

Intimacy

I can usually tell how well a marriage is doing by how frequently a couple is having sex. If there are no medical issues you should strive for at least 2-3 times per week. Because some couples have a traveling spouse, you may have to get creative with your sexual endeavors by including phone sex of some kind, but there should be a consistent healthy amount of sexual interaction. Some people read 2-3 times per week and thought, "that is impossible," but the truth is that it is very possible. One way to increase the frequency of sex is to examine your overall attitude toward intimacy.

Intimacy is more than just a sexual act. Intimacy leads to sex, but it should be an ongoing conversation in your relationship, expressed through glances at your lover, gentle touches, passionate kisses, whispers in each other's ears, and other forms of communication that let them know they are special to you. When there is a lack of intimacy conversation, there is usually a lack of sex as well. Let us discuss the origins of intimacy.

Most fruits grow from seeds, but pineapples grow from a root system that is embedded in their structure. The crown, or green leafy part of the pineapple, transforms into a root system that you plant in the ground and nurture with soil and water until it blooms into a beautiful juicy sweet pineapple. In any relationship where amazing sex is difficult, there is nutrition that can make it great. Your root system and what you require are already encoded in your DNA; all you need are the proper nutrients to thrive.

The flavorful pineapple is the result of good soil and consistent watering. What are the soil and water that feed your sex life to keep it exciting and healthy? Intimacy is a foundation for good sex. It begins before you get into bed, on top of the washing machine, or into the shower. Intimacy begins with a suggestive text message, a seductive glance, or a soft, seemingly unintentional touch. Everyone nowadays has a million and one things going on at any given time. Wearing multiple hats as an employee, parent, spouse, caregiver, and business owner doesn't even begin to define some of the roles many of us fill on a daily basis, so it's no surprise that we only make time for intimacy after we've tucked ourselves into bed at the end of the day. The issue is that this is drowning out your sexual life. I'm not saying you should sit around thinking about sex all day, but you should consider the opportunities for pleasure you have in between your many roles. Intimacy is the lifestyle that leads to good sex, not the act of sex. Sending naughty photos and suggestive text messages is fun, but true intimacy is experienced through vulnerability in front of your partner.

When was the last time you and your partner had an open discussion about how you both feel about everything? Places where you feel you haven't succeeded, things that make you feel self-conscious about your appearance, and ways you wish you could be a better partner to them? When was the last time you felt like your partner could not only see you but also see inside of you? What are the flaws you mask well to others but you don't feel the need to hide in front of your partner because you're each other's safest place? What have you said or done to show your partner that you are their safe haven? Once you've begun to rebuild the roots of intimacy, you can begin to prioritize sex again, which begins with a question. What is the source of your No?

For some women, it all boils down to a desire to sleep. Rest is like the pot of gold at the end of the rainbow, everyone has heard about but no one has seen. So, when she has a spare second, she thinks about rest rather than sex. When you do not want to have sex, it is not always because you do not want intimacy. It sometimes just isn't a priority. The thing is, once someone has committed to having their sexual desires met through you, you must make it a priority at some point.

When you think about it, most of the time when you say no to your partner, it's not because you don't want to have sex with them, but because you want to do something else instead. It could be taking a nap, completing a work project, or even writing a book about having more sex. On a perfect day, you can roll over fully refreshed from a long night's sleep and start the day with a nice orgasm. Most days, however, you're woken up by the alarm, which informs you that you've hit the snooze button one too many times. The point is that there is no such thing as a perfect moment. You just have to make it a priority, break the habit of thinking you don't want to, and consider what else is going through your mind that you'd rather be doing. Find a way to manage your time so that having sex does not feel like an inconvenience. Also, discuss with your partner how they can help lighten your load so you have more time for each other.

Exercise 4A: Rebuilding Intimacy

With the lights turned on, you and your lover should strip naked. If you want, you can use candles, but there should be enough light for you to see each other clearly. Respond to the following questions:

1. What one aspect of yourself would you change if you could?
2. What would you do if you could only do one thing to improve our relationship?
3. Why did you choose to spend your life with me?
4. What part of your body do you prefer to be touched the most?
5. Where do you enjoy being kissed the most?

Exercise 4B: Rebuilding Intimacy

1.) Engage in a conversation. If things are to improve, both parties must recognize and admit that they are not where they could be.

2.) Establish a deadline. Stop doing dishes, put the kids to bed, turn off the laptop and phone and ceasing work for the day, will help you prioritize time together.

3.) Discuss your sex life. What do you enjoy about the times you do spend together, and what perplexes you?

4.) Provide a signal. If I do this, it means that I want it. Your signal could be a specific piece of clothing you wear or a phrase you say. It can be difficult for people, particularly women, to express their desire for sex. Having a signal can help break the ice for what she may not be able to express verbally.

5.) Make a note of it when you have sex. The person who wants it the least can go days, if not weeks, without it and still feel as if you did it yesterday. A calendar aids both of you in seeing reality.

CHAPTER 6

Conversations About sex

Communication is an important aspect of great sex. It's not just what you say, but also when you say it. For a variety of reasons, the best time to tell your partner you want to do something different is not immediately after you finish. To begin with, if you have just finished, both of you, or at least one of you, should be exhausted. And receiving even constructive criticism when you are tired is not the best time. Also, if you are dissatisfied and are lying next to someone who appears to have gotten everything they desired, your frustration will most likely cause things to go awry. So, when should you give constructive criticism, and how should you do it? Begin with a compliment.

Nobody wants to believe that they are doing everything incorrectly. Even if your partner appears to be completely lost, there is something positive you can say about the experience, whether it's reflecting on how attracted you are to them or simply expressing how much you appreciate that they make time for you all to be intimate together. Decide on something nice to say, and then insert the pivot. "I love that you are so intentional about making time for us to be intimate together," then pivot to, "I think it would be even more exciting if we played a game to lead into sex, like... (insert something you've always wanted to try)." That simple sentence introduced the foreplay that you may require to get into the mood without criticizing your partner. Another example might be, "I really enjoy it when you do (insert a position you enjoy); I would love it if we did that more often." With this statement, you've just helped your partner understand what you're looking for, and a good partner will go out of their way to do what they know you like.

Some issues, such as a particular position that causes you discomfort or pain, should be addressed head on. If it's painful, make sure it's not a lubrication problem, which we'll go over later. Sex should not be painful, and if it is, you will not want to do it. Your partner does not wish to cause you harm. Some positions may take some time to get used to depending on your partner's length and girth as your bodies learn to adapt to each other or if things have shifted after childbirth. That's normal; if you communicate, your partner will understand. If something hurts during an intimate session, express it right away. You don't have to put up with it. This will only lead to you being apprehensive about having future intimate moments.

Again, if something makes you uncomfortable because of a previous experience or for any other reason, confront it. Intimacy entails more than just sex; it entails being able to be completely vulnerable with the person with whom you are having sex. Don't just ignore it; talk to your partner and seek professional help if necessary. Counseling or seeing a therapist is often regarded as unnecessary in the church, but there are people God has endowed with the gift of helping people overcome past traumas who have been professionally trained. There is nothing wrong with seeking assistance.

Nonverbal communication is another excellent mode of communication. During sex, nonverbal communication is best for conveying what you like or dislike. If you're already in the act, saying I don't like that can throw a wrench in the works. Sliding someone's hand from one place to another, on the other hand, is an excellent redirect. This is especially useful for "hand jobs." Instead of saying, "a little to the left, wait more right, now go up some, but slow down, just put your hand on top of theirs and guide them," You can take your hand away once they've gotten the hang of it. Finally, you can give instructions during sex as long as you do so in an affirming tone. "I like it when you touch my "____," or "Hold me close," and so on. You know what you're thinking; just ask them to do it. Don't say, "I don't like ____, so ____," Simply begin with what you want to happen and leave the "I don't like" conversation for another time.

When they don't get the hint, how do you bring up the dislikes? Assume your partner is doing something weird. It's not painful or triggering; it's just random and odd, and you don't like it. Even after all of your verbal and nonverbal affirming and redirecting conversations, they find a way to do these "things." Here's an easy way to deal with it. First, you must draw their attention to it, which I recommend doing in the form of a question. "I notice you frequently do ___; what do you like about that?" Understanding why someone likes something can make it less strange, tolerable, or even enjoyable. When you ask, they may say they are only doing it because they thought you would enjoy it. If their explanation makes you reconsider what they're doing, that's great; if not, explain why it makes you uncomfortable or why you don't like it. You may believe you do not owe them an explanation, but when you are in a relationship with someone, you do. You have agreed to exclusively share your bodies with one another, and that means they get all of their sexual desires fulfilled with you. If something is off-limits, you should at least tell them why. Maybe you can talk about building up to it, or maybe they can understand why it's off the table and let it go—either way, a conversation has to happen.

Now I'd like to take a detour and discuss what you should say during sex. Silent sex is perplexing. No talking, no moaning, just silence doesn't give your partner any indication of whether or not you are enjoying what is going on, and this applies to both men and women. Talking during sex should be used primarily to enhance the mood with your words. You don't have to be concerned about how it will sound because it should sound like you. You don't have to change your personality. Don't say anything that you're not willing to do. If you say you want to taste it, be prepared to do so. Even if it's three nights later, your partner will remember what you said, and even if they don't ask you to do it right away, you will need to do it eventually.

What you say doesn't have to be particularly freaky; after all, what is freaky?

It should reflect how you are feeling at the time. Say his name, tell her you like what she's doing, tell him what you want him to do next, and most importantly, tell them you love them and their body. Men, you can tell her she's beautiful and that you like the way she feels. If she's hugging you, say it's tight, so she knows her kegels are working. Discuss each other's soft skin and nice eyes. There is so much to say. Just be careful not to mumble. Nothing ruins a good mood like someone asking, "What? Huh? I don't understand what you're saying." Say whatever you want, but say it with confidence!

Moaning is another excellent sex communication technique. When they hit the right spots, you should moan and groan. This is very affirming. Let your man know he's working hard, and let your woman know her efforts to improve her fellatio are paying off. When you don't know what to say but want to break the silence in the room, moaning is ideal. It should not be forced, and it is acceptable to begin with quiet moans and work your way up to being louder and more expressive. Moaning and talking during sex should be another way to express your feelings for your lover.

Exercise 5

If you've never spoken to your partner during sex, the prospect may be intimidating. Having a conversation with them before sex to help you relax in the moment may be helpful.

What are some words that describe how you feel while having sex with your partner?

_____
_____
_____
_____

What are some things you'd like your partner to do more of when you're intimate?

_____
_____
_____
_____

What do you want your partner to say to you while you're having sex?

_____
_____

CHAPTER 7

Set the mood

The longer you've spent with someone, the more important it is to set the mood, not because you have to, but because it is what keeps things interesting. If you are not intentional about the encounter you want to have with your partner, life gets busy, kids get involved, and sex can become just another part of your day. Playing your favorite slow jams versus your high school twerk playlist will result in two very different outcomes in the bedroom. Setting the mood intentionally allows your partner to mentally prepare for what you want to experience sexually. Setting the mood begins well before foreplay. Sometimes everything just falls into place and you have the most amazing encounter with your partner, but if you want epic sex, you need to start planning early.

It is critical to understand how to turn your partner on. Does your wife appreciate flowers or acts of service? Will she think about you all day if you kiss her passionately on the neck as she leaves for work? Maybe your husband enjoys it when you slide into his DM and say something about his most recent post or send a picture that makes him have to hide his phone. You are aware of your partner's turn-ons, and if you are not, you will be by the time you finish this book. The point is that you should plan for what you want. Make sure you have the ingredients to bake the cake you're craving!

Tips for getting in the Mood:

1. Put the children to bed and the pets away! The door should be closed and locked. I understand that locking the door is difficult when you have small children because they may require your assistance, but it must be done. Glancing at the door every few minutes to see if they are looking is not a good strategy. You've put them to sleep, so trust that they're sleeping.

2. What happened to making a playlist to help you get into the mood? If things are so hot and heavy that you don't want to interrupt the flow, don't stop. However, if you're looking to set the mood, think back to the days when you'd make a playlist of your favorite love songs and let it play. Remember that the songs you choose will set the tone for the experience you want to have.

3. When was the last time you performed a dance for your significant other? Yes, gentlemen, your lady may appreciate a sexy dance from you as well!

4. Foreplay begins before touching! A wink at the dinner table or a text message at work can make a big difference. Find ways to engage in foreplay that don't include touching.

5. Get the props ready! Candles, lingerie, body oils, and sex toys are all available! Ladies, wearing something seductive will make you want to do something sexy! After a shower, ditch the granny panties in favor of a lace thong or a cute negligee with no panties at all. Allow your lingerie to get you in the mood even if your man says he just

wants you naked. Also, if you wear your lingerie BEFORE you get into bed, he will appreciate it more. Put it on while you're cooking dinner or watching TV on the couch with him. Men enjoy lingerie. Most of the time they're just thinking, "Why did you wait to put this on right before I'm going to take it off?"

6. Build anticipation. Men enjoy the buildup. And, whether you realize it or not, you do as well! What can you do at the start of the day to make you and your partner anticipate an intimate moment you can share later?

Exercise 6

What turns my partner on?

She says she is going commando
Love It**Hate it****Don't Care**

He pulls your panties to the side instead of taking them off
Love It**Hate it****Don't Care**

Kisses on the neck
Love It**Hate it****Don't Care**

French kissing
Lots of Tongue**Some Tongue****No Tongue**

Foot rubs
Love It**Hate it****Don't Care**

Full body massage

Love It   **Hate it**   **Don't Care**

Lingerie worn around the house
Love It   **Hate it**   **Don't Care**

Sexy text messages
Love It   **Hate it**   **Don't Care**

Sexy texts with photos
Love It   **Hate it**   **Don't Care**

Caressing each other in passing
Love It   **Hate it**   **Don't Care**

CHAPTER 8

Best I Ever Had

If life is a box of chocolates, sex is a field of pineapples. Each experience is distinct and flavorful, packed with sweet juices that linger and leave you wanting more. And I don't mean that each partner is unique; I mean that each encounter, even if it is with the same person over and over, can be unique. Boredom and sex should be an oxymoron. There are far too many slight changes that can be made to elicit a completely different feeling or sense of arousal. And, as with the pineapple, it all begins with a good root.

If you want to have the best sex you've ever had, stop faking it! This is true for both men and women. They will continue to do something if you constantly pretend you like it! Your partner's goal is to please you, so if you scream to the heavens that they are blowing your mind, they will continue to do the same thing, and you will be disappointed every time. Don't go mute because silent sex is horrible, but also don't exaggerate. You have a lifetime to learn about each other's bodies and experiment with new and different things, and you don't have to be afraid of awkward moments when things don't go as planned because you're in it together. This realization frees you from the pressure to be the best, allowing you to become the best.

Ladies, instead of attempting to become his fantasy, focus on being the best thing he can experience in this reality! Men, don't be concerned about comparing yourself to the last guy; operate with the certainty that she wants you to be her guy. So what if you're not freaky. I strongly dislike it when people say someone is freaky or not freaky in bed because it's so subjective. What one person finds strange may be completely normal to another couple, and it could be as simple as they like elbows and you don't. Now some of you are wondering what people are doing with their elbows in the bedroom. I have no idea, that's something I made up, but I'm sure someone somewhere is doing something with elbows because they tried something and liked it. The goal of sex isn't to be bizarre. It is to do things that both you and your partner enjoy. Being the best does not imply being the craziest, most flexible, or wildest. It all comes down to how well you and your partner serve each other.

What distinguishes you as the best someone has ever had? It's actually quite simple, but it depends on the individual. You can't put a blanket over sexual experience and say everyone wants X, Y, and Z, even though as Christians, we tend to try and blanket almost everything. Your sexual experience with your partner should be as intimate and personal as your relationship with God.

Don't Go Chasing Unicorns!

Sex is fascinating because even those who have the most amazing sex can find themselves seeking more. Not because they don't enjoy what they have, but because there's always the possibility of discovering what else is out there. I'm here to tell you that there are only so many different ways to twist, bend, and rotate your body, so don't go chasing unicorns! The unicorn is the unknown thing you believe is missing from your sex life that everyone else is aware of except you. A toxic unicorn is worse than a regular unicorn because it is the belief that another person possesses the magical key to amazing sex and that your partner is the problem.

If your sex life is good, enjoy it! You've arrived if you and your partner have orgasms on a regular basis, and no one is bored LOL. Seriously, it's always exciting to try something new, but there's nothing wrong with sticking to what you know, and you shouldn't let others convince you otherwise. It's fine if you and your spouse always end up in similar positions. It's perfectly fine if you don't want to use any sex toys, lube, or anything else. What matters is that what is going on works for BOTH of you!

Three Types of Sex

For a seasoned couple, I divide sex into three categories. Work sex, happy hour sex, and after party sex. Work sex is like when you have a job that you really enjoy, but sometimes you still want to sleep in and not go, but you only have a limited number of vacation days, so you drag yourself out of bed and go to work. You know there are only so many times you can say "not tonight" in a relationship before it becomes an issue. It's not that you don't enjoy sex; you do, and you know you will once you start. You just don't want to do it all the time.

Happy hour sex is like getting together with friends for half-price appetizers. It will be enjoyable, and you will receive excellent value at a low cost. It's most likely a quickie, which is good because it keeps things spicy. Your partner brushed you in the perfect spot or went to kiss you goodbye, but their lips landed on your neck instead of your cheek, and now everyone is late for work. Happy hour sex is unexpected, fun, and always worthwhile.

After-party sex is the "best I've ever had" sex! It's when sexual tension has been building, not necessarily because you haven't been having sex, but more likely because you had such a satisfying experience the last time that you've been fantasizing about it ever since. Or your partner has been sending you signals all day, preparing you for what's going to happen when the kids go to bed. After-party sex is where you take anything that happens normally to the next level! That doesn't mean it's insane sex. It could simply be that you are looking deeper into each other's eyes, or it could be that you all are trying out a new position on your bucket list.

What I want to emphasize is that all three of these types of sex are acceptable and have a place in a relationship. Work sex represents your commitment to not only doing things your way when you feel like it, but to also fulfilling and serving your partner's needs. Sometimes the woman is in the mood when the man isn't, and vice versa. Happy hour sex fosters spontaneity, which keeps your relationship vibrant and fulfilling even when life's routines become mundane. After-party sex allows you to step outside of your comfort zone and try something new and exciting with your partner.

You can become so accustomed to doing life together and developing a routine that you create standing sex appointments without even realizing it. It may appear strange, but it happens quickly. Monday is a no-go because that's the day your kids have the most homework, or you're mentally exhausted because you just got slammed with all the unfinished projects from last week at work. On Tuesdays, you go out to happy hour with your coworkers, and by the time you get home, everyone is asleep. You go to church on Wednesday, so you're exhausted from the running around it takes to get everywhere you need to be on time. You can finally have sex on Thursday! You could have sex on Friday, but you already did it on Thursday, so you'll pass. Saturday is sex day once more! Sunday is a no-go because you're washing, meal prepping, and trying to get a good night's sleep before the new week begins.

    Maybe your schedule isn't exactly like this because you don't have children or have a report due at work on Monday, but you get the idea. Life moves quickly, which can force you into routines you didn't intend to be in. When schedules get crazy, scheduled sex isn't always bad because it leaves room for hope, but no one wants to proposition sex, and the response is, it's not Thursday. People unknowingly fall into these schedules, robbing them of the spontaneity of their sex lives! If you want to return to the spontaneity of sex in order to increase or add excitement to your sex life, you must revert back to making sex a priority! Making everyday an option is the first step!

Tips for Amazing Sex

1. Begin fresh; it makes no difference who has previously been with whom. Even the way you all kiss each other should be a one-of-a-kind experience that you create together.

2. Discover what they like. Statements like "all girls like" and "all guys like" are not good places to start. Orgasms are the only thing that all women and all men will like.

3. Develop your ability to experiment. Experiment with different positions to see what works best for the two of you. I'll list some resources to help you get started later, but the key is to experiment.

4. Attempt to achieve orgasm for both of you. This can be difficult at first due to the female body's complexity, but once you learn the right spots, it's like having orgasms on demand.

5. Sexual Desire! A big part of having a good sexual experience is both people wanting to

be in the moment. If your partner constantly feels the need to persuade or bargain with you in order to have sex, the situation is already a "let me hurry up and finish" situation.

6. Be engaged. Show up, and also show out! It's not fun to just lay there. Sex should be enjoyable. Consider what you can do from your current position to improve the situation. What are your most distracting thoughts when it comes to intimacy? Dishes, laundry, and work? Take care of everything that's distracting first.

7. Foreplay, foreplay, foreplay. Building anticipation for a moment improves it significantly. It prepares your mind and body to engage with the present moment as well as what's to come.

Exercise 7

1. What is a position you always wanted to try?
2. If I dressed up as anything, what would you want me to be?
3. What is currently your favorite position?
4. What about me turns you on the most?
5. Which of my body parts is your favorite?
6. What is your favorite position to have an orgasm?
7. What turns you off?
8. What distracts you when having sex?
9. What mentality prepares you to have sex?
10. If I wasn't worried about_____I could focus more on our intimate moments together.
11. I am a little self-conscious about this part of my body. (Sometimes, what is distracting you is invisible to your partner).
12. I love it when you___.

13. This may sound a little weird, but I'd like it if____.

CHAPTER 9

Oral Sex

Oral sex is perfectly acceptable! It is entirely up to you and your partner whether or not to engage in oral sex, and it is completely you all's decision. Some Christian men refuse to allow their wives to perform oral sex because they believe it will be disrespectful to her, but there are numerous oral sex positions that do not involve a woman on her knees. Oral sex is not disrespectful and can frequently cause enjoyment and arousal for both the giver and the receiver at the same time, even when 69 is not occurring. The premise of 69 is a position in which the man and woman lay foot to head and orally pleasure each other.

Oral sex for men is referred to as fellatio, and oral sex for women is referred to as cunnilingus. Oral sex is when you use your mouth and tongue to please your partner's genitals. I'm going to give some general guidelines for men and women who want to have oral sex with their partner. Don't assume that just because you've been doing it for a while it means you already know what to do and don't need to read this. This is not a chapter to be skipped!

Men, here are a few things you should not do when giving oral sex to your partner. First and foremost, do not concentrate on entering the vaginal canal. Some men can, but because the g-spot is 3 inches inside the vagina, many will be unable to reach it with their tongue. This isn't to say you can't do it, but you shouldn't make it your primary mission. To elicit more pleasure, move your tongue in circular motions around her vaginal opening and dip inside every now and then.

Don't be sloppy. Be strategic. Since the nerves in a woman's genital area are more precise than those in a man's, most women require pressure applied in a specific location using the tip of the tongue rather than the thrust of a full tongue without precision.

Don't limit yourself. Use your fingers as well as your mouth. Great oral sex for a man frequently involves the use of hands, and the same is true for a woman. While using your tongue in one area, stimulate her with your hands in another, either on her genitalia or elsewhere on her body, such as her nipples.

DO **NOT** blow into her vaginal canal. It could be life threatening. I'm not making this up! It is uncommon, but blowing into a woman's vagina can result in an air embolism, which can lead to a stroke, heart attack, or death. This is uncommon and more likely to occur under certain conditions, but to be safe, gently blow around the vagina but not into it.

Many of you have probably heard of the woman who holds an ice cube in her mouth while giving oral sex (if you haven't, you're welcome), but I'd like to challenge the men to do the same to their partner the next time they have oral sex. You can use the ice on her outer labia to create sensations that are out of this world.

Ladies! Deepthroating is a technique, not the only option. Don't ruin the moment by complaining about your throat and mouth hurting if you haven't mastered it. You can make your man enjoy every blow job you give him by making him feel like you enjoy doing it. Discover a method that allows you to enjoy pleasing your man. It's about creating pressure rather than deepthroating. Concentrate on making your mouth feel like a vaginal canal. Suck firmly to simulate the tight sensation, and move your tongue to mimic its ridges. Because your lips are similar to the labia, keep them moist and move them like you would when chewing with your mouth closed. Why not just put it in the vagina? The reason is that your mouth creates a completely different experience.

Don't overlook the scrotum. Realizing your man has more pleasure points than just his penis shaft is one thing that will elevate an average oral sex experience to the next level. If you're new to them, start with a gentle graze with your fingers while you enjoy his penis with your mouth, or lick them softly while running your lubricated hand up and down the shaft of his penis. It's not rocket science, but it will have a significant impact. Using your hand during oral sex also provides a break for your mouth. You can concentrate on the tip and sucking under the tip (frenulum) while engaging the shaft with your lubricated hand.

Avoid anything spicy. I'm referring to spices like garlic and curry. If you know your partner is going to go down on you tonight, put down the onions and pick up the pineapples for their sake. This is especially true for women, but it is also true for men, because there will usually be a leakage of pre-ejaculate, also known as pre-cum, before you all move on to whatever is next during oral sex.

Ladies, instead of a simple moan, make deep humming noises to encourage a vibrating sensation in your throat, which will be a nice treat for him. Lastly, no biting! If your guy is into it, you can graze the shaft of the penis with your teeth, but don't bite him.

Now I'll discuss what to eat to slightly alter the taste of men's ejaculation and a woman's vagina. Before you say it doesn't matter because you don't swallow or have oral sex, consider this: what you taste like is an indicator of the PH balance of your bodily secretions, and your PH balance can affect your fertility and how a woman's body responds to a male's ejaculation.

The research on this topic is limited because it's difficult to make money by telling people to eat pineapples to sweeten their bodily excretions, so when you see things that say diet affecting ejaculation taste hasn't been medically proven, it's because large medical conglomerates haven't done most testing because they haven't figured out how to charge you for simple natural remedies, but lots of testing has been performed by smaller medical professionals that prove diet is a huge factor!

A proper diet will improve the taste your partner experiences as well as the way sperm affects the vagina, just as a good diet will make your skin glow and increase your energy levels. Consuming vitamin C-rich fruits, drinking plenty of water, and having clean genitalia are all excellent natural options. Lubricants are another option. Some women simply dislike the taste of skin. Flavored lubricants are widely available on the market and can be purchased online or at your local adult store.

Exercise 8

Answer these questions and share the answers with your partner

When it comes to oral sex I'm:
Interested   Not open to it   Not sure

I want to have more oral sex than we currently do
Yes   No

Something that makes me apprehensive about performing oral sex is

_____

_____

_____

I think oral sex is:

disrespectful   I'm not sure   Great

What position or new position would you like to try for oral sex?

CHAPTER 10

Moisture 101

I truly believe that one of the greatest disservices we have made to women around the world by not discussing sex in the Christian community is failing to inform men that the woman's vaginal canal must be thoroughly lubricated before he can enter it. This small piece of missing information has resulted in physically and psychologically traumatic experiences for women all over the world. When the term "wet" is used to describe the vagina, it is not a reference to water. It refers to the moisture produced by the vagina. The more a woman is aroused, the more moisture she produces, which is why foreplay is so important. You can't have enjoyable sex if the woman isn't wet. Some women may have moisture issues, which I will address shortly, but DO NOT attempt to have dry sex! Ladies, always communicate with your partner when you are physically ready or if additional foreplay is required.

Moisture is produced by all healthy vaginas! Your vagina should be moist even if you are not sexually active or aroused. Let's get started. Moisture is essential to the vagina for a variety of reasons. The lubrication produced aids in the cleanliness of the vagina. Did you know that the vaginal organ is self- cleaning? Furthermore, if you are sexually active, vaginal moisture helps protect it from injury such as tearing. The vagina produces primarily two types of moisture.

Your cervix's wetness is composed of carbohydrates, protein, and amino acids. This is the moisture that is normally very light and performs the self-cleaning that I mentioned. The other is moisture produced by the Bartholin and Skene glands. The Bartholin glands are very small and are located on the left and right sides of the vagina. Hormones play a significant role in vaginal moisture. One of the most common causes of vaginal dryness is a lack of estrogen. If you believe you have low estrogen, talk to your doctor about taking a supplement. Infections, birth control, or other medications could all be causing you to be dry.

Vaginal dryness is not only an issue if you are sexually active because, again, you want the moisture that helps keep things clean in either case. Vaginal dryness can also be bothersome. You might even misdiagnose vaginal dryness as a yeast infection. However, even the average super healthy vagina is not always wet. Throughout the month, things change.

Vaginal Moisture Cycle

Things start to feel desert-like right after your period. It's fairly dry, and if there's any moisture, it's thick and sticky. This is normally not an infection, but rather a normal part of your moisture cycle.

Moisture that is stretchy and smooth like a raw egg white is in the next phase because everything feels balanced. This is probably the most comfortable time in the moisture cycle. It's not so wet that you need a pantyliner, but it's also not so dry that you're uncomfortable. It's ideal, which sperm apparently agrees with because sperm can survive in this type of fluid for up to 5-7 DAYS! I know I just gave someone an ah-ha moment. That's how you became pregnant. The sperm went inside and just sat there!

The following period is when you are most fertile! Your moisture is wet, slippery, almost clear, and slightly irritating. This is the point at which you may decide to use a pantyliner even though you don't have to. A nice pair of cotton underwear will absorb the moisture properly. To avoid an infection, make sure you change your underwear as needed based on your moisture level.

If you have sex right after your menstrual period, you will most likely be dryer than usual. Use a natural water- based lubricant to combat the dryness. There is nothing wrong with using lube when it is needed. If you want to use this time to try something fruity and fun, make sure to wash thoroughly afterward and keep track of what might irritate you. If you are aware that you are highly sensitive to scents, avoid using anything with a scent.

To get things wet, some couples use natural moisture, also known as spit. If you choose this option, you should keep in mind that bacteria carried by spit can aggravate the PH in the vagina. If your man has a cold, the flu, or any other type of virus at the time, do not allow him to spit on or into your vagina, or on his penis and place it in your vagina. Simply grab some lube. Do not try to have dry sex. This can cause irritation that lasts for days after you've done the deed.

Keep in mind that certain lubricants can reduce the effectiveness of condoms. Read the labels on your lubricants if you use condoms as your primary method of birth control. When you're pregnant, your hormones are all over the place, so it's possible you will experience more moisture in general.

Do you want to know what natural remedies can help you increase vaginal moisture? Water! Most women believe they are dry due to arousal issues or other factors, but they only drink one glass of water per day. If you anticipate a steamy night, make sure you are drinking the recommended amount of water that day, if not more. Not juice, soda, or coffee... WATER! You can also consume pineapples or other vitamin C-rich fruits. I'm sure you're wondering why I'm obsessed with water and pineapples, but can you blame me? In my opinion, it ranks right up there with Apple Cider Vinegar when it comes to vaginal health. The high Vitamin C content of pineapples and other citrus fruits has been shown in studies to improve vaginal lubrication even in menopausal women, especially when combined with a zinc supplement! So drink plenty of water and eat plenty of pineapples, or a fruit high in vitamin C of your choice!

CHAPTER 11

A Guided Tour

If you ask your man where your clitoris is and he doesn't know, you've got a problem. It's also a problem if you don't know where your clitoris is as a woman. That doesn't mean the sex hasn't been good; it just means he's stumbled upon success but hasn't put a plan in place to ensure it. Due to a lack of understanding of the female body, boys used to take barely moistened fingers and push them into a vaginal canal. Allow me to enlighten you: that is not what women want.

Finger play is best performed in a circular motion revolving over the clitoris with clean, well- trimmed fingernails. If you want to go down to the canal and get some moisture before returning to the clitoris, by all means do so. However, the emphasis should be on the clitoris!

Check that both your and your partner's hands are clean and that his nails are trimmed. Before beginning, always wet your fingers with saliva or a lubricant. Begin around the clitoris by lubricating the fingers by touching the vaginal lips, inner thigh, and vaginal opening. Don't dive in headfirst. Allow the anticipation of what you're about to do to grow.

Exercise 9

1. Put your hand on top of your partner's and move it to your clitoris. Put two fingers on top of his and guide his movements. Slide your two fingers up and down or back and forth on the clitoral hood and clitoris. This is an excellent way to assist your man in discovering exactly what you like. Together, establish a good rhythm and pressure level, and when you are about to orgasm, move your hand and let him finish the job.

2. Tap the clitoris and hood, starting slowly and increasing in speed. The key to this is to keep the pressure low, as if he is accidentally touching you there. This tease, combined with some kissing or licking in other areas, will send you to the moon!

3. The dry hump! Take it all the way back to before you started having sex.

Straddle him and grind against his body. This is best done while wearing clothing. What incredible foreplay! The friction from you all's clothing brushing against your clitoris will create enough tension for an explosive release.

4. Apply clinched pressure to the clitoris with the index and middle fingers. Begin at the bottom and have your man tug his fingers up to the top.

5. Have your man move his penis up and down your clitoris. Use lube and have him apply pressure, but no cheating; he won't be able to go inside until you climax.

6. Get the vibrator out. As the climax approaches, lightly hoover the vibrator over the clitoris, applying light pressure. You can also begin

with a low speed and gradually increase it as the moment becomes more intense.

A word about toys: Sex is both physical and mental. You will achieve an orgasm much faster if you use a vibrator than if you are manually stimulated. Don't become so hooked on using a toy that you can't be satisfied by natural touch. Toys are a fun addition, but you don't want them to be required for climaxing, which they aren't. If you are unable to be patient, you may start to believe that you require the assistance of a vibrator when you do not. I wouldn't recommend using a vibrator more than once a week if you only have sex 3-4 times a week. Furthermore, single ladies do not use vibrators with a frequency that will interfere with your future man's ability to please you, because he is not a machine.

Ladies, if you don't know what a frenulum is, you probably skipped some sections of the book, but if you've never heard of it before getting this book, I'm not surprised because they tell women even less than they tell men. We're about to talk about how to give someone a hand job. Simply put, a hand job is when you use only your hands to please your man. The penis has many pleasure points and a variety of ways to activate each of them.

Moisture is the most important component of a great hand job! Moisture, whether internal or external, is an important component of sexual activity. Make sure your hands and the penis shaft are moisturized before beginning any hand job. Depending on you and your partner's preferences, you can use store-bought lubricant or saliva. Use enough lubricant to allow your hand to easily slide up and down the penis shaft. Your hand job may begin to feel like a carpet burn if there is no moisture present.

1. Just as the woman placed her hand on top in the previous exercise, the man should do the same. Allow your lady to get a sense of

the rhythm you prefer when getting a hand job. Do you prefer to start slowly and then pick up the pace, or do you go all in from the start?

2. Two hands are preferable to one. You can slide them up and down the penis shaft in a wrench-like motion. Using two hands allows you to get more coverage, and thus making the moment more enjoyable.

3. Gently graze the frenulum with the thumb. Slide your hand or hands up and down, engaging the frenulum, which is located on the bottom side of the penis where the head and shaft of the penis connect.

4. Involve the testicles with your other hand. Because the testicle sacks are sensitive, it is critical not to over squeeze them as you increase the speed and

pressure on the shaft of the penis. Simply palm them and massage them lightly.

5. Use your tongue to tempt him. Yes, this is a hand job, but keeping him guessing whether or not it will lead to oral sex will send him over the moon. Teasing him with the tip of your tongue will also add moisture.

6. Slide your hand up and down the shaft of the penis. Instead of going straight back down, each time you reach the top, swirl your hand around the top of the penis head, then slide back down the penis shaft and repeat.

Hand jobs are great because they can be used as a teaching tool, they can be done in a way that allows your partner to completely focus on your needs, or they can be done in a way that allows you to play with yourself with one hand while pleasing your partner with the other. This can be the grand finale when penetrative sex is not an option, or the beginning of a night full of other pleasures. Hand jobs also provide you with a hands-on opportunity to become acquainted with your partner's body parts.

CHAPTER 12

Sex positions

I'll be releasing another book full of sex positions for you and your partner to try, but for now, I wanted to get you started with some of the fundamentals.

Small Penis

When erect, the average penis size is 5.2 inches. This doesn't mean much unless you suddenly realized that the problem in your love life is that you've been trying to do the wrong positions. Size isn't everything, and I'm about to prove it by sharing some incredible positions that have been suggested for men who may be smaller- than-average in stature. But, first and foremost, size can be a sensitive subject for a man, so find ways to make your man feel secure even if he does fall into this category. If you can't think of anything to say, I'm sure the moans will speak for themselves once you try these positions.

Position 1: The Big L

Getting the woman's legs out of the way will make it easier to enter. While lying on her back, she should extend one of her legs over her man's shoulder and the other leg out to form an L shape. For easier entry, the male can straddle the woman with his legs, and a pillow can be used to elevate her pelvis if necessary.

Position 2: From the back

The woman can get down on all fours for this position, with her man behind her. She then needs to lower her chest to the bed and arch her backside upward. Envision a cat stretching and pointing its butt to the air, that is how you should be arched.

Position 3: Up and Over

This position is ideal for those seeking more adventure! The woman will roll onto her back and raise her legs behind her head. The man will squat over her to gain access and will continue to squat to thrust. For support, he can place his hands on either side of the woman or on the headboard.

Position 4: Cowgirl

The woman is on top in this position. This is advantageous because the woman can ensure that the penis remains in the vaginal canal while allowing for deeper penetration. If the woman leans in close, she can use clitoral stimulation to increase arousal. To avoid slippage, move in a circular motion or side to side instead of going up and down.

Large Penis

If you have a well-endowed partner, the first thing you should know is that lubrication is essential. The second thing you should be aware of is the existence of cervical bruising. Cervical bruising can occur when a well endowed man repeatedly hits your cervix during deep penetrating sex positions.

Sex Position 1: Reverse Cowgirl

Reverse cowgirl is the same as regular cowgirl, but you spin it around. This can be a fun way for the woman to maintain control while providing her man with a great view from behind.

Sex Position 2: Spooning

Spooning can be used for more than just cuddling; it can also be used for sex! For this position, the man can lie in the spooning position next to the woman and enter her from behind. If her man's length allows, the woman can lift her top leg up and over his top leg for added fun.

Sex Position 3: Twist Up

The Twist-up is a great position to try that will also increase intimacy. The woman can sit on her man while they are face to face and wrap her legs around his back. The man should be sitting with his legs crossed underneath her.

Sex Position 4: The G Slide

Because the g-spot is only a few inches inside the vagina, the g-slide is a fun position that can also serve as a game. As he enters you, have your man get down on his knees and you lie on your side. The trick is that only the tip of the penis enters you. See how long he can resist entering you fully, only stimulating your g-spot until he can't help but dive in.

The size of a penis is frequently debated, but what about a shallow vagina? A shallow vagina is not the same as a tight vagina. Your vaginal canal is not too narrow for sexual activity. It was intended to expand, which is why babies can emerge from it. If there is anything to be concerned about in terms of your vagina's ability to expand, your doctor will let you know. When the depth of the vaginal canal is short it is referred to as a shallow vagina. Sex can be painful if you have a shallow vagina because your partner repeatedly hits your cervix.

Sex Position 1: Flat Mission

The missionary position, in which the man enters the woman from on top while she lies on the bed, is ideal for someone with a shallow vagina. The key to comfort with a shallow vagina in this position is for the woman to lie flat on the bed with her legs flat on the bed.

Sex Position 2 & 3: Cowgirl/ Spooning

The spooning and cowgirl positions described above are also excellent positions to practice. The cowgirl position is especially advantageous because you can control the depth of penetration.

It's important to remember that with sex, the slightest twist or turn can transform a boring moment into an exciting one or a pleasurable moment into a painful one. You should speak up if something hurts or does not feel right. Sex should be enjoyable for both parties. If you're a female who is new to sex or returning to action after a period of celibacy, don't be afraid to ask your partner to take it slow and make sure you're wet enough to have a pleasurable experience.

CHAPTER 13

Introducing New Things

There is a way to introduce new things whether you and your partner are new or have been hitting the sheets for years. Pulling out sex toys at random or inserting your tongue into your partner's ear during sex isn't random in your mind, but it is shocking to them and can either intensify or kill the mood immediately. Not to mention that the more you do things that confuse your partner because you haven't talked about it first, the less safe your space becomes. So, how do you introduce your partner to that new thing that might be a little strange but you've always wanted to try? Have a discussion.

The previous chapter's exercise provided a starting point for understanding what you and your partner might enjoy. An open mind is the best way to begin a conversation. You want to be pleased during a sexual encounter, but you also want to please your partner. Listen, even if there is something they are interested in that you cannot imagine doing. Inquire as to what aspects of that particular position pique their interest. Is it the view they'll have of your body? Is it something they believe will stimulate a different part of their body? Is it just that it appears cool? Consider why you don't want to. Will it allow them to see a part of your body that you try to conceal because of an insecurity? Have you ever had a traumatic sexual experience as a result of the position that triggered you? If the latter is the case, you should be open with your partner because you should be able to be honest with someone to whom you are entrusting your body, and God is fine with you getting the help you require. He has sent people to earth who are gifted at guiding others through traumatic experiences; these people are known as therapists. Use them if necessary.

When deciding what new things to introduce, consider the following questions. Is what I'm thinking about going against the rules of our relationship? If you're in a committed relationship and ask for a threesome, you'll probably get an emphatic no, and I wouldn't blame them. Is it possible that what I'm asking will make my partner feel disrespected? For example, again, I know that traditionally, oral sex, especially when performed by a woman on a man, has been considered disrespectful by some.

Another question to ask when introducing new things is, "Where did I get this idea?" This is an important question, especially if you have previously watched porn. Simply because a large number of people have done something, does not indicate that it is a good thing. If the goal of this is to bring you both pleasure and increase intimacy, that is usually a good place to start; any other goal is not.

The best time to bring something new up, depending on the nature of the request, is not during sex or an argument. That may appear to be common sense, but common sense is not always common for everyone, and I want to make sure you all succeed. The first thing you should do is introduce the conversation. It can be awkward to go from discussing last night's basketball game to delving into sex without transitioning.

Inform your partner that you have been thinking about your sex life and would like to discuss it. Begin by affirming them. It is critical that your partner understands they are not doing everything incorrectly. Consider what you enjoy and tell them about it. This is especially important if you're going to tell them things you don't want them to do again because you don't like it.

Once you've established the direction of the conversation and affirmed them, a great way to begin presenting what you want to try is through questions. For example, you could say, "something I've been thinking would be fun to try is __" or "I was thinking it could take intimacy to a whole new level if we _____, what do you think?" Understand that if your partner believes everything is already amazing, their first question will most likely be why, and you should be prepared to answer that and, because I just want to, is generally not going to cut it.

Also, if you're considering introducing vibrators, feathers, or other tools into the bedroom, you should be able to discuss the specific context in which they'll be used. This could be an agreement that they will only be used when both of you are present or when your partner is traveling. Your agreement and dynamic will be one-of-a-kind and unique to your relationship. In addition, if your partner is unsure of their ability to please you, I would advise against presenting additional tools in the bedroom. Your primary source of pleasure should be your partner, with any additional tools serving as icing on the cake that we are so intentionally baking.

Remember that "not now" does not indicate "never", unless it does. Some things your partner will refuse to do, which is fine and there should be an explanation for every no. This is significant because when you are in an exclusive relationship, you have committed to not seeking sexual fulfillment from anyone else. If your partner wants to try something and you say no, you should explain why. Giving them a reason makes them feel better about your unwillingness and promotes greater transparency in your relationship. Sometimes a no is simply not right now.

Certain sexual experiences necessitate a high level of vulnerability, and you may not be there yet for a number of reasons. That doesn't mean you won't get there eventually. You should pray about it if it is something you truly desire, it comes from a healthy place, and does not violate the boundaries of your relationship. Because of all this sex talk, I'm sure you almost forgot this was a Christian book, but prayer truly does change things. Ask God to show you how to create a safe space for your partner to feel more at ease, or to help you understand why you should let that particular desire go or set it aside for the time being. Do not put your partner under pressure to do something they do not want to do. Don't try to persuade your partner to do something they don't want to do, and don't compare what others are doing to what you're not doing. Conversations about sex are healthy; comparing your sex life to that of others is not.

CHAPTER 14

Tips and Tricks

This section is intended to provide you with some helpful hints that you may not be aware of. This is not a list of expert skills because the purpose of this book is to cover some of the fundamentals of sex. There is much more that could be said, and much of it will be said in the workbook that will accompany this book that I am currently working on.

First Timers: If you're a woman and this is your first time having sex, don't worry. The same notion applies when you go to the gynecologist and they ask you to relax before inserting the speculum. When you stiffen up, your vaginal walls constrict, making penetration more difficult. If necessary, apply additional lubricant and proceed slowly. You have nothing to be concerned about because your body will not break.

Do Not Compare: Why is "don't compare" under tips and tricks? Comparing your sex life to someone else's will lead to its demise! One of the best pieces of advice I can give is to make sure you and your partner are having orgasms and to ignore the unicorns!

Location. Location. Location: Your home is your oyster, whether it's the couch, the kitchen counter, the washing machine, or a tabletop! Of course, sanitization is essential both before and after, but changing the location, even if it's just to the bedroom floor, is often a great way to take it up a notch.

Reach Back: While your man penetrates you in the "doggy-style" position, lay your upper body down flat and reach around to the back to spread your buttock cheeks apart to allow for deeper penetration.

Swirl: Swirl your tongue from the base to the tip to create a different sensation when doing fellatio.

Do Kegels: Kegels are fantastic! They can help tighten your vaginal walls, allowing you to feel your partner more deeply and experience more explosive orgasms. While your man is ejaculating, perform Kegels. This will heighten his orgasm and prolong the pleasurable moment.

Tips for DeepThroating: Allow your tongue to fall back and relax. You can train yourself to go deeper and deeper each time. There's no need to rush; you'll be together for the rest of your lives. Also, make sure your mouth is well-moisturized. It will make it easier for the shaft of the penis to glide deeper.

Feathers, Handcuffs, and toys: It is not necessary for every toy in the bedroom to be a vibrator. Take a trip to the sex store with your lover and find some fun things for both of you!

Cowgirl Plus: Don't focus on sitting straight up while on top; instead, lay your body to the left or right of your partner and move only your buttocks up and down. Gentlemen, you can increase the motion by grabbing your lady's buttocks and moving it with her.

Ocean waves: When your man is on top, you don't have to just lay there. Lift your pelvis slightly off the bed and roll it in sync with his thrust like an ocean wave.

Throw It Back: When you're doggy style and your guy says throw it back, don't move your entire body. Make sure you're in the proper arched position and focus on only "throwing" your buttocks back.

Stretch: The more flexible you are, the more positions you can enjoy! I'll be releasing a book soon to accompany this one, full of fun positions for you and your partner to try.

Can He Feel It: Check to see if your energy is being put to good use. You don't want to waste your time and energy on things your partner isn't even aware of. Check in with them to see if they understand what you're doing, especially if you're trying something new or don't hear them moaning as much as you think they should. Remember that sex is all about communication.

The Wrap Around: Wrap your arms and legs around your partner and pull him in closer to you as he's about to ejaculate.

Never Ending Oral: Nobody wants to be down there for the rest of their lives. Even those who enjoy giving orals want to get to the main event, whether it's ejaculation or moving on to penetrative sex, at some point. Try to be mindful of how long you put your partner to work. You don't want them to say no the next time because of how long they had to do it the last time.

Give: If you want to improve your oral sex skills, you should practice the tips I discussed, and if you want to get more oral sex, you should give more oral sex. It's really that simple. If this is your first time or you have not done it recently, it is normal for your mouth, tongue, or jaw area to be sore after oral sex. Some women have even reported throat tenderness. The more you engage in oral sex, the less likely this is to occur. You're working new muscles, so give them some time to adjust.

Know Your Turn-Offs: Know what irritates you and communicate this to your partner. Nobody wants to be shut down while having sex. If something makes you uncomfortable, just say so right away.

CHAPTER 15

Healthy Sex Habits

Vagina Maintenance

If you have sex, there are certain things you should do on a regular basis to take care of your vagina. Men don't skip over this chapter because if you want to engage your private parts with a vagina, you should understand what a healthy vagina entails and do your part to keep it that way. This starts with you, the male, ensuring that you clean your body and fingers before interacting in any way with the vagina or clitoris. Make sure your nails are neatly groomed and that the underneath is clean. If you're not circumcised, make sure to lift and shift your foreskin as needed to fully clean everything.

Landscaping

Ladies and gentlemen pubic hair should be maintained. Do not ignore this area. Your partner will have a preference, so you can obtain those specifics from them, but simply allowing things to evolve into a tangled mess is never the solution. Whether you are a trimmer, edger, a waxer who prefers to keep things as smooth as a baby's bottom or prefers to flaunt a natural bush, keep in mind that you must be mindful of how you maintain everything and it should appear maintained.

Hygiene

Use two washcloths, one for your vagina and one for the rest of your body, or get a new washcloth everyday. The reason for this is that if you wash your vagina first and your bottom last, when you get back in the shower, the first thing you do is touch your vagina with the washcloth that last touched your butt. You may have rinsed it after washing, but that is not always enough. The same is true for loofahs and sponges. Cross-contamination is your vagina's worst enemy. Along the same lines, if you engage in any sexual activity that involves the anus, that should be your last stop, or you should thoroughly clean anything that was inserted into or around the anus before returning to the vagina. Scented soaps are also bad for your vagina. Your vagina is self-cleaning and does not require soap or douching. Simply wash it with water and save the scented items for the rest of your body.

Before entering, make sure everything that goes into your vagina is clean—fingers, a penis, toys, literally everything. Also, unless your hands are clean, do not touch yourself. Before you have sex, make sure your partner has showered, especially if he is prone to sweating and/or has a lot of pubic hair. Sometimes your vaginal PH or bacterial level is thrown off, and you get an infection because your man is not sensitive to what your body requires to stay healthy. Conversation is essential! If you have recurring infections, talk to your partner about what changes you can make to improve your vaginal health. Seek medical attention if nothing improves.

Structure

The best way to take care of your vagina is to appreciate it! Whether you are abstaining from sex or are currently active, make sure that anything, and I mean anything, that enters your vagina is worthy of entry and will respect the structure of your beautiful female anatomy, whether it is a penis, sex toy, finger, or anything else.

Even though the vagina is a muscle with great elasticity, it can become loose if not properly cared for. Do not be afraid to tell a man if you believe they are violating your vaginal temple. There are also plenty of sex toys available that are larger than the average size penis. I would recommend against purchasing oversized sex toys! Purchasing oversized sex toys intended for vaginal penetration will result in a less satisfying experience with your partner. If you indulge, err on the side of caution and use something smaller.

Let It Breathe

There's a reason why the lady in the commercial says, "cotton is the fabric of our lives," not only because she's promoting cotton, but also because cotton is the best material for your vagina. Cotton underwear is breathable and will not irritate your sensitive areas. If you wear lace underwear or any other fabric, make sure it has a cotton lining in the crotch to keep the vagina comfortable if it will be worn for an extended period of time. Sometimes the best thing you can do for your lady parts is to remove your underwear and let it breathe! Simply put on a nice slip or loose-fitting shorts before going to bed.

After Sex Clean Up

Nothing starts a day better than a nice orgasm! Am I right? Of course, I am. Whether you enjoy a morning pick-me-up, a nighttime escapade, or both, cleaning up afterward is critical. Just as your vagina has a PH balance, so does your man's sperm. A vaginal PH balance should be between 3.8 and 4.5. Sperm has an average PH balance of 7.2 - 8. That's a significant leap. Sleeping after sex without properly cleaning yourself can result in a slew of issues. Whether your man ejaculated in you or not, you must thoroughly clean the area with a clean washcloth or bath sponge. If you experience fluid leakage during the first half of the day or when you get back into bed, you may want to wear a pantyliner. These fluids are made up of your and your partner's secretions. Douching is unnecessary and frequently causes more harm than good.

Sex after Childbirth

This is something your doctor has already told you, but it bears repeating. Wait! Allow your body the time it requires to recover from childbirth. Waiting the appropriate amount of time reduces the risk of infection and allows your vaginal muscles to reset. I understand if you don't enjoy working out, but keeping it tight is essential and kegels will help with this.

Kegels are a pelvic floor strengthening exercise that is beneficial to both men and women. Stopping your pee midstream is the best way to figure out which muscle to tighten. The same muscle you're clenching is used for Kegels. Kegels can be performed by women with or without a Ben Wa ball. Kegels can be done correctly by tightening your pelvic floor muscles for about 5 seconds and then releasing. Repeat 10 times more to complete one set three times a day. As you strengthen your pelvic floor muscles, your orgasms will become more powerful.

Rediscover

It is unrealistic to believe that someone will give birth and nothing will change. The same spot where your man got you pregnant may not feel the same way after you've had a baby. Allow yourself and your partner time to rediscover your body following birth. Determine which areas still tingle for you and which no longer do. The nipples may have been your thing in the past, but they may have gone numb after months of breastfeeding.

Keep in mind the section on erogenous zones. See if you can try any of those areas or incorporate hot and cold sensations to help activate things again. Your hormones are fluctuating, which has an impact on your sex drive, but you can mentally prepare yourself for success. Attempting to get more rest by having your partner assist with the baby will go a long way. An exhausted mind is not an aroused mind. Try getting into a relaxed state and begin to envision you and your partners sex highlight reel to get you into the mood.

Make a new intimate space for you and your partner. When the baby is constantly in the bed, it becomes a shared space. If you are not yet ready to move the baby to their own room, or if they have returned after being kicked out, you should make a space for the two of you. Where can you and your partner meet up around the house that can be designated as your space? What about the laundry room, the kitchen pantry, or a guest bedroom? It may sound absurd, but a change of scenery can do wonders for your mind. Also, be deliberate in setting the mood and extending the foreplay. Consume more water if you are nursing to ensure you have plenty of moisture available after feeding the baby.

Communication will be essential because a man is prone to doing what he did last time that worked. Discuss what feels different. Make it a point to slowly rediscover your vulva together. Set aside some special time just to rediscover and explore. Your new favorite position might be something you've never tried before.

Bacterial Vaginosis

The dreaded BV (Bacterial Vaginosis) conversation is upon us. I am 99% sure that every woman has either had BV or known someone that has had BV. BV is NOT an STD, and it does NOT mean you do not bathe! BV is an infection, just like yeast in the vagina can become an infection. BV is caused by an overgrowth of bacteria in the vagina. All vaginas naturally have bacteria in them.

Signs of BV

There is a foul odor. Even if it is that time of the month, smelling like fish or old eggs in your vagina is not normal. There will often be a thin, grayish discharge. I discussed discharge in the chapter on moisture, so please refer to that if necessary, but keep in mind that discharge is normal. You'll know if your discharge is a symptom of BV because it smells bad. Normal discharge does not have a distinct odor. BV can sometimes cause pain during sex, or the pungent odor will be amplified during or after sex.

How to Prevent BV

Maintain good hygiene by wiping from front to back, showering daily, and wearing clean underwear. Allow nothing dirty (hands, men, toys, 'whatever') inside your vagina. Take shallow organic apple cider vinegar (ACV) baths before your period if you notice a pattern of BV whenever it's that time of the month. Always remember to contact your doctor if strange smells or discharge are coming from your vagina because I'm not one.

Yeast Infections

As embarrassing as it is to admit, most women, particularly those who are sexually active, have had a yeast infection before. Wait a minute, if it's that common, it's not at all embarrassing! To begin with, a yeast infection is NOT an STD! Second, yeast can be transmitted through sexual contact. I know I just confused some of you, so bear with me while I explain.

A yeast infection simply means that your vagina's PH balance is out of whack, causing your vagina to produce an excessive amount of yeast. This can happen even if you've never had sex. Also, if you have sex while suffering from a yeast infection, you can pass the yeast overgrowth to your partner, who can then pass it back to you. Men, if you have jock itch and have sex with your partner, it can present itself like a yeast infection in your partner.

Signs of a yeast infection

A severe itching sensation that will not go away. An odorless, clumpy, thick discharge or a very watery discharge. During sex, there is often a burning sensation, as well as redness and swelling.

How to Avoid Yeast infections

Always make an effort to keep it dry down there. Yeast thrives in warm, moist environments, so be sure to change your underwear after engaging in physical activity. If you have a yeast infection, avoid having sex. The friction from a condom could aggravate the situation, and if you don't use one, you can spread it to your partner, who will then give it to you. In the vaginal area, avoid using scented soaps, lubricants, or food items. All of these factors can upset your vagina's delicate balance. If you really want to try having sex, be sure to cleanse immediately after with a mild unscented soap or warm water. If you are unsure of what may be happening, always reach out to a professional health care provider because I am not one.

Urinary Tract Infections (UTI)

When your urine burns so badly that you suspect you have an STD but don't. A UTI is also known as the honeymooner's disease, which is misleading because a UTI can occur even if you have never had sex. UTIs can affect both men and women. It is not an STD, and you will not pass it on to your partner, but having sex with a UTI can be painful. A UTI is no joke, as anyone who has had one will tell you! UTIs are classified into three types: bladder, kidney, and urethra. The symptoms of a UTI are usually mild and barely noticeable at first, which is what gets people into trouble.

Signs of a UTI

Pelvic pain that feels crampy. Having the urge to pee but producing little to no urine, cloudy urine, strongly smelling urine, and a burning sensation when urinating.

How to Avoid UTISs

Drink plenty of water and cranberry juice. Not the sugary, mixed-flavor one, the nasty, bitter one from the health food store.

In any case, seek medical attention from a professional to determine your best course of action. I'm not a medical professional.

140

In Conclusion

Sex is a fantastic world to explore. What you'll experience with your partner will be unique to the two of you. The more intentional you are about developing intimacy, finding and rediscovering each other's bodies, and seeking to satisfy each other, the better and more orgasmic your sex life together will be.

Do not be afraid to try new things and be a part of helping other Christians transform the way they think about, discuss, and experience sex. If your sex life becomes stagnant, pick up this book again and repeat some of the exercises to rekindle the spark.